Repeat the Flesh in Numbers

Kris Bigalk

NŸ Books™

The New York Quarterly Foundation, Inc.
New York, New York

NYQ Books™ is an imprint of The New York Quarterly Foundation, Inc.

The New York Quarterly Foundation, Inc.
P. O. Box 2015
Old Chelsea Station
New York, NY 10113

www.nyqbooks.org

First Edition

Set in New Baskerville

Layout and Design by Caroline Evans
Cover photo from "A Voice Within—The Lake Superior Nudes"
by Craig Blacklock | www.blacklockgallery.com

Library of Congress Control Number: 2011940336

ISBN: 978-1-935520-54-2

Repeat the Flesh in Numbers

Acknowledgments

"Repeat the flesh in numbers" appeared in *Water~Stone Review*; "Mistress" and "Confession" appeared in *Dust and Fire*; "Three Parables of a Breakdown" appeared in *Marginalia*; "The Abandoned Mind," "Insomnia" and "Previous Tenant" appeared in *Caveat Lector;* "Birthday" and "My Husband, the Architect" appeared in *The Binnacle*; "The Alternate" appeared in *The Bare Root Review*; "Graveside Service" appeared in *Main Channel Voices*; "Expecting" appeared in *Ribbons*; "New Year's Eve" appeared in *14 by 14*; "Pest Control" appeared in *Mead: a journal of literature and libations*; "Absolution" and "If you leave me" appeared in *The Minnetonka Review*; "Taliesen Burning" and "Housewife" appeared in *Modern English Tanka*; "Ghost Story" appeared in *Forge*; "Trailer Park Cinderella" appeared in *the cream city review*; "Emily Said" appeared in *The New York Quarterly*; "'My Dogs Are My Kids,' She Said, and I Said" and "Headshot" are forthcoming in *The New York Quarterly*; "I Do Not Care for Fear" appeared in *The Iron Horse Literary Review*; "You think love is" appeared in *Pank*; "Refinishing" appeared in *Rag-Mag*; "Aren, Two Years Old, Playing at Orchard Park" appeared in *Silk Road* and *Hip Mama*; "Mr. Spock Always Gets Stuck in Aisle 13—Cereal and Breakfast Items" appeared in *Rougarou*; "Señor Squirrel" appeared in *Pif*; "Comatose" is forthcoming in *The Great Twin Cities Poetry Read 2011: An Anthology* (Lowbrow Press)

Contents

II. This Paper We Call Skin

III. Before We Knew Our Names

I. Repeat the Flesh in Numbers

Repeat the flesh in numbers

cell by cell, gene switches
flipped, tripping along like
a Bach fugue, a Hanon exercise,
precision tempered with passion,
a practiced virtuosity that eventually
falls apart slowly, as the
joints stiffen, bones pull apart.
Muscles loosen like stretched
rubber bands—all you learned—
practice makes perfect, for example—
proven so ultimately wrong, for in
the end cells practice themselves
to ruin, to death, to dissolution.
This is the ultimate perfection, then,
to practice until the music needs
to change, to dissolve into silence,
so that the music has something
to hold itself against, like a child
asleep, held up by a tree root,
dirt, and grass, its breath audible
only when the wind is still,
the air heavy with rain.

Repeat the flesh in letters

Repeat the flesh in letters
D, N, A, a helix of imagined
perfection, twisted around a rope
of good intentions, a Jacob's ladder
empty of wrestling angels, just a weak
rung here or there—cancer, an immunodeficiency,
diabetes, high cholesterol, and the stumble
down begins, the falling towards (or away)
from (or to) this mathematical grammar
that makes me who I think I am, the glue
that sticks my soul to my cells, into one
being, me, the imperfect, the mortal,
setting my ladder down as my son
takes his up, the generation
that pushes forward (or back)
one more inch.

Last Year's Lilies

Their heads bowed, brown, like
paper bags frozen into the snow
stark, stiff, holding firm as rigor mortis,
brown in one light, gray in another,
a heart-sized bulb beating underground,
tiny roots, spider veins, fed by
melting icicles. Often
we ignore the dead, but these clutch
at us so openly—they rise in spring winds,
small flags, dessicated, they stare
askance—dust and dark defined,
posing like art models, limbs lithe
and fragile, genitals arranged
carefully, faces turned away.

The Gardener

Your brown, grass-stained shoes, side by side, near the chair,
Your red flannel shirt draped on a hook, like a shawl,
the smell of fresh-cut grass floats gold-green in the air—
summer's last growth before the hardest frost falls.
Shirtless in the garden, you kneel barefoot, tug at weeds,
roses and chrysanthemums all spent and bent down,
nothing left on stems except husks emptied of seeds,
and still you wrench and wrestle dandelions from the ground,
shake the dirt off, and throw the leavings in a heap.
You will make this bed perfect, with clean-edged bare borders,
each clump of quack-grass excised, roots ripped.
You find peace in this work, bringing chaos to order,
a man whose air castles have solid foundations,
who weeds this love's garden with experienced patience.

Drink the Dark Out

There is an order, a right way
to fall apart, and I learned quickly.
A whirring, like hummingbirds, then
deep blackness sinking into my stomach.
I found my small wish dashed to pieces
like a favorite tea cup, and I relive the instant
it slipped away from my fingers. It returns
each moment my hands are not busy.
It waits for me to scold or shake,
but I won't. I can't help but welcome
this sinking.

As I drink the dark out
more takes its place,
the cup never emptied
on this day when the
sun never sets.
Steps sound on the street
cobbles, loud as bells,
and I remember that lightness
in the steps of the old me,
the one so filled with brightness
she almost floated.

The Abandoned Mind

You have to understand
this mind was a burden;
I didn't really want it.
Keeping such a psyche healthy
is not a one-person job,
and I was so young.
It just appeared one day—
I didn't even know
I'd been carrying
it inside my head, thought the
extra weight of my thoughts
was just another migraine
gone wrong.
I didn't know it would cry
so much, keep me up all night,
demand every minute
of my time, wanting to be fed,
needing to be changed...
Lord, more than an hour
without a change and that mind
would stink up the whole house.
Sometimes it just cried
for no reason at all.
It got to be too much
for a girl like me to handle.
That mind drove me to drink.
Towards the end, all I could afford
was cheap vodka.
It would sleep for awhile,
but wake up screaming
louder than ever.
Finally, one night after the booze
made it warm and sleepy,
I set my thoughts on the steps of a church,
wrapped in an old quilt.
I left no note or instructions.
What would I have said,
anyway?

Birthday

My mother remembers that my father went
to get a haircut while she labored, and
in the same minutes the cord between us
was snipped with stainless steel scissors,
my father's hair was shaved tight
against his head, his beard lopped
by a straight razor, the foam hitting
the floor, speckled with stubble.

Freshly washed, body trembling,
lungs burning, wrapped up
like a present for him, swaddled
in a pink blanket, I was waiting
on a young man with horn-rimmed
glasses and freshly-shorn hair, whistling
down the street with *Life*
magazine tucked under his arm, expecting
to meet his first-born son.

The Alternate

When I was thirteen, I rode the bus home
from school, the bumps jostling my shoulders,
worrying the day's conversations through
my head. I had pimples, my dishwater blonde
hair was stringy, I didn't own a pair
of Calvin Klein jeans like Brooke Shields,
and besides, a thick pair of cotton underwear
came between me and my Levi's every day.
My older sister, smooth-skinned, raven-haired, sat
in the back of the bus, let a boy rest his hand
on her knee, rolled her eyes if she caught
me looking, the boy snickering
until my cheeks stained.

When we got home, my sister took
the telephone and went to her room,
locking the door. I took down the 22 rifle
and loaded it with shells, walked out
the back door, flicked off the safety, and sighted
on the blackbird that perched on the tip-tops
of the spruce trees behind our house, the trees
that towered between me and the rolling
cornfields, the trees that sheltered us
from the road, from the round headlights
of passing cars, from the wind
that blew hard against their branches,
turning into whispers.

I set the rifle to my shoulder,
fit it into that tender slot between socket
and collarbone, squinted my left eye,
lined up the ball between the forked
sight, then focused everything on that stupid
blackbird's head, and squeezed, slight,
slight, until the tension blew back,
the hammer threw, and the blackbird
dropped through evergreen branches
like a stone.

Birds Drop from the Sky

They fell heavy as coal
from gray, high clouds,
punching the frosty dead
grass with black feathers
and bruises of blood.
Angels felled mid-flight,
on the way to nowhere,
and they landed nowhere
in particular, a rain of
blackbirds, oiled, desperate.

I dreamed that night
of walking down the city street,
people falling lifeless down stairways,
slumping over steering wheels,
tumbling off bicycles, streetlights
still clicking colors on schedule,
my head ringing with a song
I replayed over and over,
my heart in my ears
like wingbeats.

Three Parables of a Breakdown

A starburst compass points me to the last light.
The night hums, twitching black edges,
a fistful of evening, too timid to knock,
slinking through the cracks like a cat.

Shadows of leaves whine as they fall,
a quaint noise the dead say is wrong.
They look into the book the world lost,
find all the answers, and judge us.

Dogs gather around, slip along the edge of day
with me, this cage of bones, looking on the bright side.
They murmur amongst themselves, certain that
Nature will meet us in this twilight,
wearing old muddy boots, smelling of lightning.

The Witch Tree, Lake Superior

The rock between us, heavy with history –
a tree clasps its outmost edge, roots like a fist,
branches threading the sky with small green fluttering.
It seems to breathe in water from the lake below,
eat from the soil that rain washes around it.
The rock is just wide enough for our hands
to stretch across, touch fingertips –
through storm and calm, branches
reaching upwards,
fists unfurled.

Exegenesis

I bleed
without permission,
without effort or injury.
I bleed prophetic, a
waterfall, a flag,
a protest, an insistence
on rest. I let go
the water I have gathered
and saved. I push out
pieces of myself, chunks
of life's materials, bedding
of fetuses, wept-out hopes,
the leavings of dreams,
the blood trail of grief.
I bleed out relief.
I bleed fear, red and
full at first, then brown,
old, chronic. I bleed now
because I can, and bleed
for the time when I can't. I bleed
passion, I bleed what couldn't be
borne, I bleed after
impossibility is birthed,
I bleed when the moon
is full, I bleed when the
tide goes out, I bleed
when I cry, I bleed
when I laugh. I
bleed without
blame, without sanction.
I bleed.

Apocryphon of Eve

There was no rib that begat me.

> My first memory is of the giant catalpa tree,
> strung with little white orchids,
> leaves big as dinner plates, trunk heavy,
> branches spreading the ground with dappled shade.

> The Lord lifted me to my feet, and He and I walked
> the paths in the Garden for days, sweet smell of the orange
> blossoms melting on our tongues, laughter
> of the angels murmuring behind us.

There was no snake, no forbidden fruit.

> In truth, I saw Lucifer once, under the catalpa,
> stringing flowers together to make a chain.
> He put it around my neck and smiled. I was afraid
> and happy all at once. I never saw him again.

> When the Lord brought Adam to me,
> cradled in His arms, still wet
> with saltwater, crying, I took him
> to the Tigris, I washed his body with my hands,
> rinsed his hair, kissed the stinging from his eyes.

There was no thirst for the knowledge of good and evil.

> I loved Adam's body, the way it fit into
> mine, how the scent of him flushed my cheeks.
> When there were no words between us,
> I liked him best. I grew fat on the taste of him.

> It was years later, as I sat at my son Abel's grave,
> I understood why the Lord was so silent
> on our walks, how he stroked his beard,
> did not meet my eyes, my every
> word, every move, every prayer,
> a disappointment.

Expecting

I carry his blood
in a drop of seawater
deep in my body.
This small ocean's tide is strong.
Its breakers crash against us.

One Last Time

The womb of tattered bedclothes
shapes of limbs turn to shadows
in the half-lit dawn—
the smell of old socks, new sweat.

One, his voice,
Two, his hands.
They repeat themselves,
wrinkled, an unwrapped ball of paper, illegible,
like the words he's forgiven, forgotten,
words he's saved to savor,
his obsession with himself.

Light, half-light, no light.

A hand over the void and there was light.

Don't forget the body's language,
he reminds me. We sing in unison,
the song buried
in the thrum, the flash
of headlights
outside the window.

A smaller darkness lies ahead,
when a road turns from dirt to mud—
where the rain takes me.

Vibrato

Tremors on a silken web
waves cresting crashing
beats resting
pitch until it holds
steady
echoes like a fugue
or chorus

breeze rushing through the door
cold with clarity
rolling across
the wood floor
the edges of my voice

lanterns glowing
dropping from
them like gold
daring you to reach
touch
tastes of curry
turmeric

filled with the blood
of animals swollen
and happy
about to burst
skid and roll
intentional and sinuous
from a pinprick

stitched up
to a minor
seventh chord.

New Year's Eve

The snow hovers, a mist of champagne bubbles
swimming down to the bottom of a flute glass.
In the blue of almost evening, the troubled
sky gnarls its brow on the skirts of the day past.
This night brings a new year, but there is no wind
to howl and scratch at the door, no gold full moon
to light the way across drifts, to clear the mind.
No confetti, no honking horns, no balloons
no Auld Lang Syne. Let's stay out here, in the yard
listen to soft sift of snow, watch it collect
on our shoes, melt on our lips, forget the canard
of the clock's twelve strikes, tense future perfect.
Peace tastes like this—pure, sweet, and cold;
it melts through our fingers, impossible to hold.

Graveside Service

There is work in wearing a red rose, its heft, its darkness.
I would like to be cold as the air, consist of a splendid clarity.

But I bear the pall, all reason lost in the snow rising behind me.

I am a guard of this corpus, this fact after woman,
after girl, the buoyancy of her body sunk

into dusty rose satin, mouth sewn into a smile.

The old ones come forward to pray, but I see only tired
hands, many hands that smell of eucalyptus lozenges.

As the pastor drones, I look up at the mourners,
black coats flapping against the sparkling white snow dust.

Aging Gracefully

I am searching for more mistakes to make—
errors in judgment, like buying two hundred rolls
of toilet paper, or impulsive blurting, telling the bag-boy
I dreamed of him last night, French-kissing a navel orange
behind my back. Errors are better than wrinkle creams, dermabrasion,
even bo-tox—they keep the face flushed, expression haunted, eyes wide,
no crow's feet visible, no smoker-wrinkles around the mouth.

Mistakes can make men follow me home. Less than
perfect is so irresistible, some sure thing to measure his dick
up to, and have it come out longer, somehow.

After I dye my hair, trying for dark auburn but getting purple,
I'll cook supper, burn the potatoes, undercook the chicken, and end
up eating half a peach filled with cottage cheese, wishing I could have
brought myself to peel that navel orange and take a big lick of it myself.

Señor Squirrel

The habenero peppers were no accident.
I grew them
especially for you,
to watch you pluck a bright yellow bonnet,
turn it over in your hands like a topaz
or tourmaline, then sink your bicuspids
hard into the flesh, only to throw
it three feet into the air, your mouth
on fire with my revenge, tail stiff
and high as you raced for your burrow
as I laughed, counting the losses
I had suffered at your paws—tulip bulbs,
sunflower heads, sleepy mornings
interrupted by your family arguments
in the tree outside my window...

Me gusto, Señor Squirrel.

Pest Control

When Arleen tells me she drowns squirrels to save
her tulips and iris from their hungry little paws,
I, impressed, thrilled, horrified, imagine the lithe,
gray body banging against the mesh of the live-trap cage
as Arleen dips it into a large tub of cold water, how its head
arches back as it hits the top, floating with its little lung
balloons, until it finally inhales the chill, falls
silent. It is more generous, she says, then driving
the cage out past the lake, freeing the brat
into the woods, where the other squirrels will taunt, bite,
starve it until it curls up under a tree root and shivers
its way to death. It is more generous, she says,
than shooting the rodent with a bb gun, maiming it, blind
with pain, until it dies in its nest from infection or blood loss.

But I am more of a coward, Arleen. When pressed, I can't
watch the final struggle, holding gently
until it's over. No, I leave loves in hospital beds, abandoned
to starvation of food or air, or surrender them, wounded
beyond repair, to the mercy of doctors and nurses—
and when it is over, they are gone, my hands clean, dry, my garden
full of perfect red tulips, frowzy purple iris, the walnut tree
heavy with green-skinned nuts.

Old Man Autumn

The west wind blew down
the flowers today, shaved
the leaves from the silver maple
like a mad barber, knocked
power lines together until
they sparked and the stoplights
faded black.

The wind smelled like snow,
but carried none,
like a father returned
home, smelling of whiskey.
The wind
blew the side door open
in the middle of the night, scattering dead
leaves and cold into the kitchen
and then lingered,
a still cloud of frosted fall
pushing into our haven,
letting us know he will come
and go as he pleases
by our leave
or not.

Centenarian

Deep in teeth and tongue, eugenic dipthong of ugliness,
sense of losing thoughts like lint from a leaky pillow.
I'm so old now the miracle of my first
breath seems ordinary, a yarn no one left alive
remembers or even thinks of. Memory is an
orbiting planet that will never reach me, elliptical,
curve slow and deep, a heavy gravitational
wave that pulls the water in my body to
and fro, that reels the asteroids and dust of thought in circles.
They will never know their courses were not
of their own choosing, never realize they are broken
off pieces of me, sent out but not quite given up, not yet,
not until the sun quenches us all with her fire, her grip.
There is always another to whom we owe our lives,
to whom we trace our entirety.

Insomnia

Tiny bones, those splinters
that form wrist, thread together foot,
little pins that hold flesh
like fabric and batting, a quilted body.
These calcium shards betray and sting,
they ache with age, say my name
while I sleep, until I wake, say
hush, hush.

The Mathematics of Dying

Lines, planes imagined
in some sterile space
rotated, spun—but
rotate infinity?
Where are the trees,
the grass? Where, except
in gardens, do vegetables grow
in perfectly straight lines, or bear
fruit on perfectly vectored branches?
Mathematics, so human
so full of its own narrow logic,
claiming God, infinite,
when infinity is the reason
to go on, charting lines
through space, from star
to star, knowing
space will
never run
out.

II. This Paper We Call Skin

Comatose

Pull me out of this wall,
spell me with letters traced on my back,
my thigh, my wrist, traced with fingertips
light as a daisy petal. Pull me out
of this plaster, this stasis, sing me out with rhymes
against the cartilage of my ears, loud as trumpets.
Pull me past the studs, the framing, conjugate
the verbs of my muscles, bend my arms until
they fold around your shoulders. Pull me from
behind the pipes and outlets, coax the words
from my throat as you would a butterfly
from its chrysalis, with slow, light presses
of the thumb, until the edge cracks, and
my first words emerge with wet wings,
fervent, trembling.

My Husband, the Architect

He has drawn me lying naked
on a square spare bed,
my hourglass hips framing
the licking fireplace,
curtainless windows.

He has drawn me into a kitchen with
square blue walls, neatly rendered
appliances, my arms held out
over a paper stove, stirring
a paper stew.

He has drawn me on the roof,
silvery shingles dancing
under my clog-clad feet.
I grasp the lightning rod,
waiting for dark clouds.

Taliesin Burning

Fire ate his dreams, scorched
gold sandstone walls, alchemized
the stones red as blood.
He set these rocks in new walls.
They catch at the eyes, like grief.

Previous Tenant

In the empty apartment, under the sink,
I find an old tea cup, ancient dregs ghost brown stain
marring the bone-white bowl, a red-orange
lipstick mark on the edge, a parting kiss.

I imagine her idle, in the early afternoon,
dripping tea on the table,
a donut crumbling in her hands.
She takes a drag from
a Virginia Slim (I found the
dusty full ashtrays on the windowsill,
hidden behind the tattered lace curtains).
She wears her pale yellow chenille robe,
a careless singe mark marring the left sleeve,
the newspaper spread like a tablecloth
before her, the light from the half-open blinds
just a little too bright.

Ghost Story

A man was haunted into me;
he smelled of charred bones and mulch,
his clothes brown and heavy,
face overgrown with hair and beard.
He inhabited me for moments only,
in the fresh dark spaces of day and night.

In morning, he cleaved the sky,
a freshly painted room
white with possibility.
After noon, he swayed in the weeds,
calling me to eat. At twilight, he sang
my name as he walked back alleys.
At night, he chanted the paper
from the walls in the guest bedroom.

One midnight, descending the stairs,
he missed a step, tumbled into
sienna shades of light,
someone else's life.

Vestige

Remember the the mask you made for me,
that caricature I strapped to my face
until I believed its lies, even spoke them aloud
through the cloying latex?
After you left, I kept it in a sticky top drawer,
where it darkened, scowled. Later,
I set a small coil of rope
next to it, like a python. At night I heard
it bumping against the lock.

I still dream, sometimes, of knotting
your feet together as you sleep,
tying your hands in front
of your crotch, strapping
that ugly version of myself
to your face, so you could see
how it felt to wake that way,
only slits of sun.

When You Leave

Take your three-day beard
                    your razor-thick wit
Take your fifth of whiskey
                    you keep in your raggedy jacket
Take your wilted Cuban
                    you dip in the whiskey and suck, a sixth wrinkled finger
Take your spare prose
                    chopped out grisly on an old Royal typewriter
Take your pistol
                    the bullets are in the medicine cabinet

Information Age

Side effect of neglect,
only time for company, overspending the day.
Pixels tingle like sleet across my face,
a false sense of mortality, of time.

Only time for company, overspending the day
as the sun rises above the white dominoes of gravestones.
A false sense of mortality, of time,
one divorce, ten years and a hysterectomy after the fact.

As the sun rises above the white dominoes of gravestones,
there is chaos in this order, blooming as my tongue blooms.
One divorce, ten years and a hysterectomy after the fact,
each curved comma a road sign, each period, a resting place.

There is chaos in this order, blooming as my tongue blooms.
Poetry, that ever-patient dog, sleeps in a corner,
each curved comma a road sign, each period, a resting place,
penetrating my bones, shaking through my arms.

Poetry, that ever-patient dog, sleeps in a corner.
Pixels tingle like sleet across my face,
penetrating my bones, shaking through my arms,
side effects of neglect.

Dr. Barbie's Abortion Clinic

Girls that party like Barbie
on the beaches of Malibu
must have that occasional
birth-control failure, have
to make a discreet visit to
Dr. Barbie, who of course
has had her own sexual adventures
and understands completely
that she needs to do her part
to make sure there is never a
Visibly Pregnant Barbie,
which would lead to a
Morning Sickness Barbie,
Stretch-Mark Barbie, and
Varicose Vein Barbie,
which (considering Ken's wayward ways)
would lead to a
Single-Mom Barbie,
Post-Partum Depression Barbie,
Lose the Baby Weight Barbie, and
Leaky Saggy Breast Barbie.
Too much reality
for a little girl to take, thinks
Dr. Barbie. If this celebration
of motherhood is really necessary,
better to skip ahead to
MILF Barbie,
Super Suburban Mom Barbie,
or, even better,
Step-Mom Trophy Wife Barbie –
that's the kind of thing
a little girl should really
set her sights on.

Trailer Park Cinderella

The children never were born.
They materialized, like fog in morning
scraped knees and knuckles
edged with tears, one exigency
after another, making step-mother
and step-sisters seem undemanding,
perhaps even kindly in their indifference.

Cindy's new once upon a time
depends on small details to continue –
tonic water, mostly, mixed
with absinthe, or gin, various
pill bottles, rattling with balm.

A crowd of bystanders will soon gather,
some forgotten, others familiar –
friend, enemy, lover, Prince –
her palm told her the future ends tonight,
and the tea leaves don't lie.

No one told the children that their happily ever after
was entirely up to her –
that the next once upon a time, this one,
begins at a kitchen
table, just after midnight,
a nine millimeter on
the table, next to the gin
and Xanax.

Housewife

she presses her hands
against her wrinkled secrets
nerves like damp laundry
in the moldy-nosed basement
waiting for starch or iron

Mistress

I take you like a bear, bite at your chest
wrestle you down, mark your back with my claws,
clutch bruise-prints on your shoulders, wrench
my body to yours 'til you growl, snort, and gnaw.
After I'm finished, I digest you for days;
the thought of you shuddering down my back
until the hunger begins again, a whispered prayer
and my ice-hard resolve suddenly cracks.
You start with those snowflake kisses round my neck
and end at the end, in a drift of desire
Icicle tears melt down my cheek.
You, my immolator, unsinged by the fire.

Does she see my bear scratches on your lovely tree?
Or do you only make hate in the daylight with me?

Remedy

Empty places scare you, those long-grass
quiet meadowlands of childhood, walking for miles
with only birds for company. You imagined everyone
you knew had slipped away, floated off to ride
clouds, sunk underground to spelunk the caverns, turned
into trees waving on the horizon. Being missed
is important, being that thought
on someone's mind that hangs on like a cockle-
burr, impossible to fully remove, always
some little fuzz or claw to remind,
frustrate, accept, or reject. But
you'd rather be a hunger, a craving,
like good dark chocolate or heavy
Swedish coffee, the kind you need before
ten o'clock each morning, or else a headache
will haunt you the rest of the day—yes, you
want to be the remedy before the symptom,
the warm blanket at the foot
of the bed, the reflection
of all who love you, perfect
versions of themselves
shining in your eyes.

Saffron Amnesia

She has fallen into
a saffron amnesia, brilliant
as the sun sinking under the cornfield
framed in the west-facing window,
thick as the pollen that coats
the windowsill, dank as an Iowa August,
and as still.

Not even the mockingbird calls
in this yellow forgetfulness;
he perches on a fencepost,
head cocked, as if listening
to music emanating from
the string of crooked barbed wire
vibrating under his feet, a tune dancing
in his bead-black eye,

and she wonders
if she could somehow break
through the window-glass, wade through
the scrub-grass ditch, grasp that rusty
spiked fence with her age-knobbed hands,
feel the thrum of it, like catgut or piano wire,
she wonders if then she could wrench
herself, palms bloodied as Christ's,
back into her body
again.

Emily said

she never ate chicken again
after sitting next to a chicken
truck in traffic, the pullets
panting in the August sun,
feathers dripping from cages
like obscene fowl sweat.

She had never had a chunk
of her skin taken out of
her hand, incised by a nasty
orange beak, never locked her
sea blue eyes with those black beadies,
evil and intent, a little cousin
of the Tyrannosaurus Rex,
a carnivore inhabiting a small-brained
jerky feather-head, just waiting
for evolution to take another turn.

No, Emily saw them posing
as fallen angels, white with fright,
legs broken. Emily didn't taste revenge
in a fried chicken leg, or a barbequed breast—
but when the juice ran down *my* chin,
it tasted so sweet, so tender.

Mr. Spock Always Gets Stuck in Aisle 13—Cereal and Breakfast Items

First, there is the choice of grain:
    corn, wheat, rice, oats, quinoa, bran, a combination?
Then, the shape:
    clusters, cubes, circles, octagons, squares, orbs, flakes, or grit
Then, the flavor:
    sweet, vanilla, frosted, chocolate, berry, honey, or nut?
Then the texture:
    puffed, dense, crumbly, crisp, soft, or crunchy?

It's hard to be a Vulcan, to know what the breadth
    of your choices are, to have no cravings
or habits to guide you,
    to know that this choice
will make no difference to anyone
    and still, he paces the rows of boxes,
finger tapping lip, one eyebrow
    arched, stomach grumbling.

"My Dogs Are My Kids," She Said, and I Said

you need to admit it's just a conversation starter
        designed to make you look
                oh, so sensitive, an animal lover.
Awwwww....Admit it
If you chained your child
        in a kennel while you
flew first class
        cross-country
charges would be filed, and show me a kid
        you can pacify with a rubber bone
There is no Doggie Social Services to
        file charges when you leave
the dog alone in the house all day
        without a sitter, just a bowl of dry
        dog food and a dirty bowl of water
and please just shut up
        about how Bowzer shredded
your $300 Jimmy Chu shoes
        for one thing, you called them your "Chu's"
and it's a lot to expect a dog
        to not hear that as "chews"
and for another thing
        if you had a kid and he had
eaten your shoes
        you're the kind of person who would put him up
        for adoption
or maybe, if you were feeling charitable, have him put
        into inpatient therapy
but a dog who chews up shoes
        is a great sympathy generator in a cocktail party
        conversation—so you keep the pup, hoping
        for more humorous anecdotes.
Admit it, if you really
        had guts you'd take the dog
to the pound
        get yourself knocked up
and really, really
        have a reason to be
miserable or maybe even
        admired.

Love Circus

I've stopped asking questions
about love, stopped trying so hard for
balance, walking the tightrope without
a pole or a net—the walking, even the falling
is worth the bruises, the broken bones, the occasional
concussion. Someone will eventually
help you up—or maybe they won't, the clowns
just munching peanuts while you bleed. In time
you will rise, stagger out of the ring,
heal. So, go ahead and practice, worry
all you like—it won't make a difference.
Falling is how we get down, and it's so
breathtaking, watching the ground
come up to meet you like a good, hard kiss.

Twenty-Four Want Ads

I.
Wanted: pair of shoes
candy-apple red satin
heels honed to a razor-sharp point

II.
Wanted: one red dress
strapless, with sequins or bling
size eight, ten, or twelve

III.
Wanted: one sober poet
with plush, moist, talented lips
hard hands with soft touch

IV.
Wanted: one drunk poet
to sleep on my couch and snore
to remind, forget

V.
Wanted: novelist
to gloss over the details
a missed period
a careless word, no matter
basking in his own brilliance

VI.
Wanted: book contract
no royalties required
no agent fees paid
just a pretty cover please
and a blurb from someone big

VII.
Wanted: new body
barter, trade or cash up-front
five-year warranty
preferred but will take three year
as long as she purrs and growls

VIII.
Wanted: a burka
the pretty blue kind, with net
to cover my eyes
I could walk the street noticed
and dismissed just as quickly

IX.
Wanted: a Coach bag
to fill with candy
cigarettes, tissues, lipstick

X.
Wanted: fountain pen
and black ink, accoutrements
of nostalgia

XI.
Wanted: a perfect child
the kind other people have
that become doctors,
lawyers, professors or shrinks,
who love you despite it all.

XII.
Wanted: a new job
no customers, no vendors
no boss, co-workers

XIII.
Wanted: a sunrise
red, orange, completely still
no cars rushing by
even the birds respectful
the sky empty of airplanes

XIV.
Wanted: a sunset
purple, blue, scented with pine
trees wishing for night

XV.
Wanted: fine cognac
warmed in a clear glass snifter
rolling over tongue
like alliterative prose
moving toward a happy end

XVI.
Wanted: one day free
of cartoons, plush dinosaurs
the alphabet song
string cheese, applesauce, yogurt
diapers, laundry, dishes, shit.

XVII.
Wanted: some self-pity
three feet, mucky and thick
so when I wallow
it clings, sticks, stains, ensuring
my reason for staying lost.

XVIII.
Wanted: flamethrower
with new training manual
and extra fuel

XIX.
Wanted: a glass house
filled with bookshelves facing out
titles pressed to panes.

XX.
Wanted: sewing kit
with extra buttons and pins
needles pre-threaded and sharp

XXI.
Wanted: religion
requiring no commitment
or self-effacement

XXII.
Wanted: a round stone
to throw into a deep thought
ripple and settle
to the unconscious sea floor
impress the clownfish and squid

XXIII.
Wanted: a cactus
blossom pink, soft and ruffled
spines poised stilettos

XXIV.
Wanted: a pair of shoes
jet-black suede kitten peep-toe
heels that click down long hallways

I Do Not Care for Fear

It tastes like hard ribbon candy
kept in a milky-glass candy dish.
I would rather kidnap Baby Jesus
from the creche, tuck him
between my teeth and cheek
His bitter paint staining
the edge of my tongue.
Don't you see Mary's hands
clasped over her heart,
adoring, adoring?

The Boy Next Door, Home from Vietnam—1976

I. Spring

Long, tall, and lean, held together by tensile wires,
he moved like a marionette, with a jerky fluidity,
crossing the pasture between our farms in a zig-zag,
sometimes crouching, sometimes standing tall,
twitching, glancing behind and scanning the road
to the East.

II. Summer

At the Bicentennial Fourth of July Celebration,
the Community Band played the national anthem.
He stood, swaying, drunk, screamed the words,
stomped his feet to "Oh say, does that star-spangled
banner yet wave," and the rest of us stopped,
so that only his cracking, sobbing voice sang,
"the home of the brave."

III. Fall

He brought me a pumpkin to carve for Halloween, carried it
across that same pasture between our farms. I sat on the back
stoop and watched as Dad's usually docile shepherd lunged,
broke her chain, and charged him. He threw the pumpkin
down, caught her in mid-air, wrestled her down as her teeth
snapped onto his arm, and he wrapped his hands around her
neck and squeezed the life out of her until Dad pulled them
apart, the dog's limp body like a rag in the grass, the boy
covered with blood and pumpkin guts, all of us fallen into an
awful silence.

IV. Winter

When I saw the police cars
idle down the snowy road, I knew it wasn't
good. His mother found him that morning
in the barn, hanging from a chain
in a far corner
away from the cattle, frozen fingers
thick icicles, his beard lacy with frost.

The Body's Garden

The cancer blossoms, little cauliflower florets,
knobby under her skin, like new cartilage,
her body trying to revise itself, to renew
those fallow places he laid to waste.

The carrying of this new life burdens her,
a difficult, constant ache. It stretches
the skin in new directions, pulls the heart
out of place. But where do we go if we don't
go forward, if we don't cultivate
the soil of our childhood, mulch it to grow
something beautiful, grotesque,
and ultimately fatal?

It moved to her forearm, the green branch
he twisted until it snapped; she used
to trace her finger over the ridged bone afterwards,
crooked, like a badly grafted vine. It was there
she first felt the seeds swell into bulbs, then,
overnight, bloom into crocus. Soon, it moved
to her breasts, turned them to lilacs, then climbed
up her back, a clematis.

This permutation is the body's way of saying
it will not be killed, but that this body will
choose its way of leaving,
remake itself, the severe art of flesh
turned to flora, grieving towards
a warm eternal sun.

What She Said

Words rush, syllables combine,
like she is speaking
a language of music
and repetition, Urdu or Farsi,
the kind of language unfamiliar,
the lift and fall of tones tell
her story, not that the story
matters, what matters is the way
her lips and mouth form themselves
around these memes you are supposed
to understand, but refuse to really hear,
your pulse like clashing cymbals
dousing your ears with rushing
invisible droplets, and her voice rises,
white-capped, a wave
breaking against your beach,
pulling you slow
into her sea.

Dinner Party

I am inviting Marilyn Monroe
to dinner this evening
and I think we will go casual
maybe have hotdogs or burgers
on the grill with some baked beans,
chips and salsa. I'll tell her to wear some
khaki shorts and a blouse, nothing expensive
because we all know about barbeque sauce
and salsa stains. She should be quite relieved
to dress down after all those photo shoots
in expensive dresses and diamond jewelry;
and I hope she'll have a couple of lite beers, settle
in on the chaise lounge,
and talk about absolutely nothing, because
if there's anything she needs, it's to forget
about presidents, diamonds, champagne,
conspiracy. We'll talk about family,
the weather, how to choose a perfectly ripe avocado
or how to make good artichoke dip
and after dinner we'll roast
marshmallows over the grill coals
and smoke cigarettes,
glowing with the fireflies.

A Night Alone

A bowl of peeled peaches,
wet, blessed fists
of sweetness that find
my mouth, my willing teeth,
hungry tongue, wounded
peach blood running
down my chin so obscene.
I am alone, free to slip out
of my terrycloth robe, let
the juice and bits of peach
flesh drizzle down my neck, between
my breasts, the sweet honey of it
sticking to my fingers.
I take a knife and slice
a long, fat finger from the last one,
its coolness so perfect, so
satisfying when I purse
my lips around it, suck
its liquor into my mouth,
and think of you.

You think love is

the stubborn sand that sticks between teeth,
grit on bone, the wash of salty saliva,

the sweet pang of a worried hangnail
held in front teeth and twisted, over and over,

the unhealing scab that dries just enough
around the edges to pick and pick and pick.

Urban Love Letter

From my car window, I see sewer grills
fill with water
roil with promise
acrid gasoline-soaked air
swarthy, badly shaven, smutty
with tar and sweat
spreading it like thick frosting
hashed criss-cross by dim lights,
rushing wheels.

You were easy to forget.
I cast off the rope
we tugged in our love war, your bright
pretense of nonchalance
in the photograph I hold, such emotion
deadly if you breathe too deep
or too long, you said,
an image you inhabit, who
you really are.

Maybe tonight you'll speak,
your voice round, brass, heavy
as a shotput glossed with water.
The grass is listening.

A broken guitar string
makes a crooked tune, ice cubes
clinking in my travel mug, gin
blooming there like gasoline encased
in plastic. Fading headlights
heavy, ponderous, caught against
the rain gutter, a circle of natural glow
blown down the alley, shining
down from your bedroom window.

Promise

Promise me you will never recall our first night
together, the quiet velvet wrestling on cool June
sheets, the air folding around us like a blanket
that we threw off and pulled back over one another
with small breathings. If you remember it without me,
it will change, ever so slight—the time of day,
the color of my dress, what we ate or didn't eat.
If we remember it together, we will change
it together, this myth of our creation, when
the sun rose on the two of us and has not since
gone down.

If you leave me,

I will carve the shape of you
from an oak tree,
every curve of your body
naked, bright.

I will smooth, burnish your skin,
caress it
with sandpaper,
stain it
the color of blood
with a fine Merlot.

In broad darkness, I
will run my hands
over your wooden
buttocks, up
the bumps of your spine,
over the smooth cut
muscles of your back.

My body will catch
fire and glow,
ember-like against your grain.

But your effigy will not smolder
in my fervor; he will stand,
eyes closed,
smile slight,
living the dreams
I've whittled
inside his head.

Absolution

I forgive the perfume of clove cigarettes
hanging from your head in curling, frazzled dreds.
Love is carrying water with no rest, despite
the alarm clock, a circle-burnt nerve, the television baby-
talking
to itself, endlessly rocking you out of your cradle.
Its shadows wrestle with the distance.

I forgive the drunken worm behind your teeth,
the way your head blooms amongst clinking glass,
a shattered stone. The blood seems ashamed
of itself, a red line, a thread.
Grace is downy, silken; it blooms
like clouds in coffee, whitens everything
it touches with its whip.

I forgive your alphabetical orders,
your pine-scented tree air fresheners,
your small-tongued secrets.
It is hard not to love the glitter,
how it sticks to your fingers,
finds its way into your panties,
scratches itself into you
like bits of sugar.

Confession

Oh bless me Father,
for after we have sinned
I stand in the corner
of the hallway where
I can see a narrow rectangle of you
between the bathroom door
and its hinges
you don't quite fit
into this narrow frame
but it draws my eye
to the angles of your shoulder blades
knifing back and forth
as you brush your teeth
the undulations of your buttocks
as you reach into the medicine cabinet
the ripples of your back
as you caress your face
with the electric razor
and I check my watch
to see if we have time
to sin again.

III. Before We Knew Our Names

Incarnation

We are born shivering
wishing back the damp warm dream
the pounding of a heart
deep rumbling ruminations.

All our lives we wash and baptize
rinse with rose water
annoint ourselves with almond oil
yearn for the lush red bed
the lemony sweet fluid
we breathed before
we knew our names.

Reincarnation

You will begin.
In this beginning,
you will sense no one,
nothing other than your body
stretching into itself like a sock, forming
a boundary between water and air, combining
so the two can seep into one another only through you.
You will see yourself as a curtain that separates wind and sea,
and when lightning cracks, singeing you together with
its hot needle, stitching you tight to this new self,
that is the moment when
the forgetting
begins.

The Organist's Daughter

A labyrinth of basso profundo floats, the lowest
note of the previous hymn a halo of buzz
around my head as I slip through
the narrow passages lined with tall
tubular pipes. I creep, following
the drone, hammer in hand, and when
I hone in on it, raise my fist and whack
against its vibrating low curses, smack
it low, on the floor, and then higher,
until the valve knocks back in its metal
throat, bellows hissing, waiting
for the postlude.

Late Dreams

I've been attending house parties
in Heaven, crashing little black dress
soirees in starlit mansions, crossing
dewy cool lawns in my bare feet, strappy sandals
dangling from one hand. I always find someone
I know (or knew), even at the Baptist mansions,
even at the Muslim mansions, even though
these are usually crawling with virgins,
who generally don't make for good conversation;
they tend to titter like birds. These mansions
have rooms upon rooms. I often lose
my purse and need to retrace my steps,
searching under every chair, checking out
the bags hanging from the arms of every
other woman, until I realize
this is Heaven, a place where
it is impossible to lose
anything.

Headshot

I needed a photo of the poet
for the Facebook invite to the poetry reading,
so I Googled her impossible Polish name
(I can say that, having my own impossible Polish name)
searching the thumbnails littering the page like confetti.
A pair of large, firm, breasts appeared, held up
by two graceful, feminine hands.

This would definitely boost attendance.

But, I thought, how to know if these breasts
were really the poet's breasts—her name appeared
in the file name, but after all,
there could be a porn star in Poland with
the same name, though these breasts did
not have the Polish porn star look about them—
they definitely looked like sheltered breasts,
taken out only for special occasions.

I began an e-mail.
Hey,
I Googled you and came across these
marvelous boobs. Are they yours?
No.
Just checking,
Is this the photo you'd like
to use to advertise the reading?
No.

So, after another long look,
I moved beyond the breasts,
scrolled until I found a photo
where I recognized the poet
with the Polish last name, her head cresting
the surface of a blue lake, her green
eyes smiling as if to say
I've got something here, under the surface
you're really going to like.

The Summer before He Came Out

He had been snapped open, cracked
like a lobster at the breastbone, jagged
scar dotted on either side where the stitches
(or was it staples?) pulled him tight again,
his heart back in place (or so they said).
He wore that scar when we went to the beach that summer
bared it when the other boys
came around, pointing to me and saying
Look, she ripped my heart out, stay away.
When really what he meant was
Come closer, the longing for those boys
so deep, so beautiful and foreign,
as if feathers had grown from his scalp,
as if his eyes had turned to opals.

She Said, "Oh, Don't Take Everything So *Personally*," and I Said

I want to take **you**
personally
you know, just me, by myself,
but you might be too heavy
for me to lift
personally;
so in order to be taken, you
may need to take yourself
seriously,
which will be difficult, I know
but please don't take that
personally,
it's more about my lack
of fitness than your obesity,
more about my humors
than your seriousness, it's nothing
personal
nothing
serious
unless you want it to be,
personally;
which will bring us back
again to your fat,
unfunny, immovable
ass.

Mother America

I.

Mother America did not breastfeed, because it would have spoiled her perfect, grapefruit-sized, tomato-firm breasts. So her children lived on milk from her cows, spiked with antibiotics, sucked on latex nipples, held on to plastic bottles, thought "this is my mother."

II.

Mother America lives in a trailer on the edge of town, works a minimum-wage job taking money at the gas station. She knows everyone in town, and they feel sorry for her, an overweight single mom, raising two ungrateful teenage boys. She hasn't bought herself a new outfit for three years. Her hair is wild, and she doesn't bother with make-up. After closing time, she sucks the cocks of her friends' husbands in the backseat of her Impala, $20 a pop, uses the money to buy some pot from the town cop, lights up, and thinks about the good old days.

III.

Mother America gets a pedicure every week and tips the Vietnamese girl $10, just to keep her loyal. Mother America has a personal trainer, a nanny, granite countertops. Mother America is at home even less often than her CEO husband. Her heels click on the sidewalk, blood-red toenails lined up like prisoners on the edge of her shoes.

IV.

Mother America is angry at her sagging belly, sad breasts, her body loved and bred to ruin, only rubble around the frame of the beauty she once was. Men built her up, then laid waste to her, and still they come to cling, to suck, to be kissed and pressed to her breast—there there, there there.

The Convent Letters

I.   April 1909

Dear Baby,
These walls that hold me in
are dark and warm, how I imagine
your prison might be. But you
may be content, you have never
known sunshine, or felt the lush grass
on your bare feet. The bars on the windows
cut lines into my face, cast shadows
on my belly where you hide,
my little fish, in a snug round bowl,
oblivious to love
and its consequences.

II.   May 1909

Dear Nurse,
If you had ever felt his tongue
between your lips, how hungry he was
to touch every inch of your body—if he
had run his hand up your skirt, all the while
staring himself into your eyes, your mind, if he
had promised you a ring, a house, a life—
maybe you would have been the one confined
here, round and fattening. Maybe you could
imagine yourself that way, and look me
in the face. Or maybe you can imagine
and it's why you don't look. See me,
this reflection of all you dare
not do.

III.   June 1909

Dear R_____,
I love you was your weapon, as deadly as a rifle,
with its long barrel burnished and oiled, bullets
packed tight with explosive words that ignite
when hammered with my questions. Your weapon,
my balm—the words mean nothing now. Love is so
human, and I have turned into an animal, Darwin's
darling. Now I know about love, its excuse for violence,
obsession, violation. But I welcomed your parting
shots, the way your face shifted when the weapon cocked,
ready to blow. Forgiveness belongs to God,
so does not concern me. We animals remember how
we got our wounds; we lick scabs long healed, worry
them with our teeth, try to flatten the scars
to fit our new skin.

IV.   July 1909

Dear Old Self,
Remember how the school floors smelled of orange
oil, the desks of bleach and lye? The woodstove blackened,
a cord of wood stacked next to it in a perfect triangle.
My desk, in front, oak, brand new, the top drawer
filled with chalk, pencils, a marking book. The blackboard
was hung in three sheets, the washmarks still visible. I wrote
my name, "Miss Serfling" in big letters, on the board right
behind my desk, so I could sit underneath my name.
This was my classroom, my domain, one place
I could be the smartest, was supposed to be
the smartest, where any boy who dared mock me
would end up on a stool in the corner, pressing
his nose against the cold wall.

V. August 1909

Dear Baby,
In order to leave this place, I must give you up.
At night I feel you roll and pitch, a boat
bobbing at the dock, or a seal frolicking. How dry
and hot this bed would seem to you, the ocean swept
away, the dock with it, and you, alone,
wailing, arms trembling, the only vestige
of one man and one woman
and the lies they told
each other.

VI. September 1909

Dear Mother,
The hills here in California are dusky
with autumn, the grape
leaves turning orange and brown, wine
crushed out of grapes like love.

I have done a terrible thing.

My belly swells like a pomegranate,
full of seed and blood.

Mother, when
you were sixteen Father swept
you away to the prairie, miles
and miles of grass blowing
in waves like a green ocean.

My lover locked me away with
the Sisters, behind heavy oak doors
with locks, no keys.

They call one nun Mother, but
her eyes are cold with Jesus
when she looks at me.

VII.   October 1909

Dear R_____,
He did not have my yellow hair or bright
Norwegian-blue eyes. His mussed black hair
curled like his clenched fingers, wet
with my blood, his green eyes round
and wide. He felt awkward in my arms
like a sack of onions. They only let
me hold him for a minute, then rushed him
down the hall, that last bloody, living
piece of what was between us, let loose
in the world like a ghost
with no address, no memory.

VIII.   November 1909

Dear Old Self,
I left you in a room,
a white-walled, hot room.
Pain strumming your distended
belly no worse than the hollow spot
where your heart used to be, throbbing
and swollen with what you thought
was love.

The moment he was born, you died.

Now, I live you in your body. He was foreign
to me, a stranger's child. I felt
no urge to hold him close, only relief
when they took him, squalling. I do not miss
you, either, Old Self, with all your crying,
all those messages you wrote
and ripped up, clogging your thoughts
with silly words, the wastebin
with your tiny curling scraps.

Self-Portrait of an Abandoned Poem

I was born without hands or hair.
They grew in late and awkward,
at angles with the other edges
of myself,
bodies, the form of thought,
are like that—born corrupted,
they can heal themselves—born
perfect, they can develop a cancer
that first sullies, then destroys,
a whipping up of flame and smoke.

I climbed out of ashes, I grew
new limbs, pink and easily bruised.

Who have you become today?
What piece of yourself will you shed
tomorrow?

The fire burns at a distance, scarlet
on the horizon long after sunset,
the smoke a taste in the air,
sweet, sticky, wet.

Dear twin,

mirror that touched my hand before I had a hand,
back when we looked like popcorn shrimp,
our bug-eyes useless in the womb-wet dark.
Being right or wrong was not important then.
You were another moon whose orbit
I occasionally crossed, who grew larger
and closer, but then, one day was gone—
then the water receded,
and the dry world of cold,
of loud, of light seemed empty
without you. They called me colicky,
but it was simple grief, my first
taste of the solitude between,
and I raged against its yawn,
yearned for the ocean
where we stood in the breakers
silent together.

What We Name

                    named (become)

unnamed (   )

The stillborn

                    unnamed (not here)

The baby who breathed

                    named (here)

became part of us and then

                    wasn't (here)

Stillborn

                    not here (medical waste bin)

Baby who breathed

                    here (cemetery)

Antiseptic, stainless steel

                    not (here)

Grassy hills, wreaths of roses

                    (here)

Their hearts stopped

                    at different moments (here)
                    and not (here)

We decided which was

                    a thing

We decided which was

                    a human

judged

                    the weight

the economics

                    of emotion.

Aren, Two Years Old, Playing at Orchard Park

When the other mothers' eyes leave their own children,
stare at him, then at me, when their small talk
carefully circles the questions they want to ask:
What is wrong with him? How did it happen?

I want to tell them how, when he was one day old,
he stopped mid-breath, lips bluing.
I touched his cheeks, puffing air against
his sweet-bowed mouth until he
sighed against my ear, until his dusky
skin turned pink again, and he agreed
to stay, but not wholly.

I want to tell them how I held
hopes, at first flickering like fireflies,
in my cupped hands, a glance
of light glinting now and then
between my fingers,
but when I opened
my palms, their gray bodies
curled up like withered prayers,
dry as paper.

I want to tell them how I wait
for the cool May nights to come this year,
how I will take him out into the
dew-flecked grass, the little sea-glass green lights
of fireflies glittering around our feet and knees,
how this time, I will catch my prayers
delicately, only for a moment, then release
them back to the lilac-scented, cricket-song night,
how I will teach him to do the same.

Despair

Here, a necessary resting place, a tent,
not a home, where I wash the dirt
from my face, the mud from my shoes,
shed the dusty clothes of an old life,
toss them aside, go naked.
Here, I write down the rules of my life
and then eat them, letter by letter,
until my mouth tastes like paper,
bitter, dry.

Here, I lose my sense of smell,
all the flowers filling the pasture
with their blank, sad faces, their scent
falling off me like snow.

Here, the sound of the wind clatters
in the tree branches, this my only music
for weeks on end, until I wonder how
that wind would feel on my nakedness.
When I breathe deeply, I catch
the scent of gardenia,
make plans to pull up stakes.

Hope

Deadened by day
resurrected by shadows
wicked dry by sunshine
bleached by desert winds
it seems that eons pass
waiting for God's breath.

So far away from here,
a cloud of sleet, or hail
full of little lives and little deaths
dares me to fight.

How undone we are in this dryness,
but we appear as we imagine
ourselves. How is it there
you widened
with excess, a wonder
and a freak, like so many
raindrops, absorbed.

I am not your mother—
but I decided to keep you,
large-eyed and hungry.
Here is a kiss—it is yours—
spend it all in one place,
a one hundred percent return
on your investment. Claim
your damp spot and occupy it, choose
the softest, the darkest, the loveliest,
you who will not return, my last
wild hope.

Brain Storm

"…and then a storm broke in my brain…"
Albert Einsten, in a letter to Besso

A storm broke
in my brain, thunder cracking
as material and spiritual
bumped against each other,
white hot bolts of intentions
threading crooked down
my spine. A storm broke
in my brain, and each second
turned infinite,
so that the God I believed in
ended up being myself, a blend
of us all, or none of us.
So many moments absent
of me, trees clapping
in the woods when no one
listens. We are wrong to call
ourselves sentient, having developed
this false sense of mortality, of time
sifting by. A storm broke
in my brain and the hail beat
its icy pellets of doubt, the rain
soaked my skin anxious, the blackness
gathered at the edges of the West
so that this moment of eerie anticipation,
so infinite, became for me only an instant
and the sun returned, the sky whatever
shade of blue I chose.

Midsommer On the Isle of Giske

When dusk comes instead of night
the old woman refuses to unseal the wax
on the letter gathering dust on the table,
preferring to eat it raw, ink running
down her chin, a necessity of time
on this island where women
don't disappear, but expand
into spaces left between.

In the faces smiling from small photographs
on whitewashed plaster walls, no one older
than thirty, a tow-headed boy pulls a red wagon,
a bearded young man dandles a baby on his knee,
a smiling young woman looks on.
Three lives that stopped when they left; smiles
difficult, unheard of, now.

The realization of mirrors
points out the window to the sea. The only
disappointment now is the weather, constant.
The fields fill with dandelion eyes
blinking yellow, then white.

The old woman says love is an effort
best left to God—
a secret kept in the child's jewelry box
with other forgotten keepsakes.

Refinishing

After she died, the grandfather
clock ticked too slowly, the snow
piled outside the window and socked
in the hours until they repeated themselves
repeated themselves, repeated themselves
like a paragraph read, re-read, and not understood.

He cleaned out the desk, filed the papers,
the bills, the receipts, the drawers no longer
jangling nail clippers against a hundred pennies,
paper clips, black hairpins, used-up ballpoints.

He searched the bathroom for fresh razor blades
until he held them shiny in his palm, blinking back
the snow light blaring from the windows.

He scraped the desk clean of its white paint, green paint,
until she shone, blonde and naked, absorbed
and reflected cold winter after fifty years
smothering under the ice
of dated colors; he ran his fingers
over her edges, smoothed, sanded her grain
dusty bright, and she almost
breathed again.

Soledad

In a house where floors
have familiar creaks, your companion
the dripping faucet, the broken
door latch, the cracked kitchen
window—because, for you, love
is a noun, never a verb.

Your solitary comfort, loneliness –
gray, wet, smelling of dog,
rests on the rocky banks
of a creek, living only in
certain moments, like a flicker of gold
glances off water, not speaking
unless spoken to.

Your memories float down
the rapids, pounded into froth
by stones and branches, into
fairytales of water and breath,
testaments of the space between two
grains of sand, measures of the time
it takes for a scrub pine
to root itself in the crevice
of a limestone bluff.

The wind pushes words back
into your lungs as you survey
the landscape, footprints and white wooden
highway crosses, the occasional tree
scarred with hashes, as if someone
had tried to mark a trail home.

Gravitas

Don't sleep too hard or fast,
let the eyes drop slow
the wrist curl towards your face,
the weight of blankets press
in, the weight of bed beneath
fall away, until you are suspended,
like you were once in the womb,
tethered only by an umbilicus back
to your mother, your unconscious.
In that floating (not falling)
there is sleep, light, slow
breathing, and then clutch,
kick—hypnic jerk
and it's done,
time to begin again.

Free falling,
air resistance meeting gravity
at ten stories so when I hit
the pavement I am relaxed
as a cat tumbling from
a tree, as nonchalant as the
ex-lover who doesn't recognize
me when he takes my order, brings
me sweet tea.

There is a warping of time, of memory
with each fall, long and short, each
tumble into infatuation colored
with the scent of cologne, a joke,
a gaze, each crash down the staircase
punctuated with a blood trail
of musings, of self-scolding.

Walking is simply falling
forward—as we grow
older, the style loses shape,
the ground not so reliable,
and so we fall to it, looking for
comfort, finding only a cold shoulder,
ready to break our bones, bruise us.
Gravity beats old with
an incessant hum,
lures us back to the dust,
invites us to sit there
think of Newton
and his apple tree,
how ridiculous
it is that we give him any credit
at all for naming it, giving it
this terrible power.

The Last Day

I want it to dawn bright,
yellow fingers of sunlight flipping
the blinds open, a hush flooded
with air underwing.

Infinity is how
we imagine it, in particles
invisible to the human eye.

Pain is a moment to savor
and forget, entrance or exit,
the same. But in utero, that dark ocean,
I imagined no dry world of light,
no mother, unaware
that the steady drumbeat above
my head was her heart, beating.

Perhaps it is the same
with the rhythms of morning,
of night, and when I wake
to the new light, there will be another
kind of mother to hold me, unimaginable light
dripping from her hair, her eyes,
my skin like sweat,
like memory.

About NYQ Books™

NYQ Books™ was established in 2009 as an imprint of The New York Quarterly Foundation, Inc. Its mission is to augment the *New York Quarterly* poetry magazine by providing an additional venue for poets already published in the magazine. A lifelong dream of NYQ's founding editor, William Packard, NYQ Books™ has been made possible by both growing foundation support and new technology that was not available during William Packard's lifetime. We are proud to present these books to you and hope that you will continue to support The New York Quarterly Foundation, Inc. and our poets and that you will enjoy these other titles from NYQ Books™:

Barbara Blatner	*The Still Position*
Amanda J. Bradley	*Hints and Allegations*
rd coleman	*beach tracks*
Joanna Crispi	*Soldier in the Grass*
Ira Joe Fisher	*Songs from an Earlier Century*
Sanford Fraser	*Tourist*
Tony Gloeggler	*The Last Lie*
Ted Jonathan	*Bones & Jokes*
Richard Kostelanetz	*Recircuits*
Iris Lee	*Urban Bird Life*
Linda Lerner	*Takes Guts and Years Sometimes*
Gordon Massman	*0.174*
Michael Montlack	*Cool Limbo*
Kevin Pilkington	*In the Eyes of a Dog*
Jim Reese	*ghost on 3rd*
F. D. Reeve	*The Puzzle Master and Other Poems*
Jackie Sheeler	*Earthquake Came to Harlem*
Jayne Lyn Stahl	*Riding with Destiny*
Shelley Stenhouse	*Impunity*
Tim Suermondt	*Just Beautiful*
Douglas Treem	*Everything so Seriously*
Oren Wagner	*Voluptuous Gloom*
Joe Weil	*The Plumber's Apprentice*
Pui Ying Wong	*Yellow Plum Season*
Fred Yannantuono	*A Boilermaker for the Lady*
Grace Zabriskie	*Poems*

Please visit our website for these and other titles:

www.nyqbooks.org

CPSIA information can be obtained at www.ICGtesting.com
Printed in the USA
LVOW102128301111

257283LV00001B/6/P